Creativity and Innovation

Accessing and optimizing your inner visionary, entrepreneur,

artist and muse.

by Tim Levy

November 2013

Title: *Creativity and Innovation*

Subtitle: *Accessing and optimizing your inner visionary, entrepreneur, artist and muse*

Author: *Tim Levy*

Published by: *Tim Levy and Associates LLC*

Second Edition, November 2013

Published in the United States of America

Dedication

This book is dedicated to my amazing and lovely family. My life would be incomplete without my Bella, Finn, Zak, Angela as well as Anita, Chris and Nicholas in Australia.

I must also thank my core team and beta-testers who have been so amazing. A special mention goes to Robin, Barbara and Amber.

Finally, thank you to everyone at Vistage, CEOSpace and Secret Knock who have been so important in these recent years.

Thank you, one and all.

Contents

SECTION ONE

Creativity and Innovation

Section One

This book begins with some details of my own personal experience with creativity and innovation in business and beyond. If you'd like to focus on the more practical tools and process, feel free to skip ahead to Section Two.

MY CREATIVE STORY

Creativity and Innovation

GREAT WORK PEOPLE,
BUT I'M JUST NOT FEELING ANY OF
THESE DESIGNS

My Creative Story

The first question that people ask me, as we begin to explore the topic of Creativity and Innovation, is 'How did you get to where you are today?'

As an author, speaker, consultant and coach I must tap into my most innovative and creative thoughts every day. It's my job to bring new thoughts, new ideas, new initiatives and strategies to my clients in every presentation, every consultation and conversation.

So how did it all begin? Did I have an unusual childhood or was it pretty much the same as everyone else's? What were the key factors that lead to my children's books, television shows and comedy routines? What was the sequence brought me to my current focus on big picture strategy, technology and content with big business CEOs and entrepreneurs of brands that you know?

Like all good books, this one begins with a story.

Elementary Creativity

Way back in elementary school, I was a voracious reader. I didn't have any real social skills at the time so I spent lots of time alone, reading books in the library. I would even take books home to read. I was kind of weird as a kid, right?!

Anyway, there was this particular series of children's books that I really loved called *The Muddle-Headed Wombat* (Ruth Park). These books were about a bumbling wombat and his friends.

Don't exactly have a picture of a wombat in your mind right now? Well, a wombat is a solid burrowing animal about a foot by two feet and built like a brick outhouse. I ran into one by mistake one time, running full speed – and I bounced off. I nearly broke my ankle. Seriously.

Anyway the wombat in the books is a kind of cartoon version that just carried me away creatively. I started to write the *new* adventures of the Muddle-Headed Wombat just for fun. The stories somehow got to my teacher who was so impressed they got *typed out*. For something to be typed out back in the day before personal computers was a huge deal! I remember they even glued my stories into the back of the *Muddle-Headed Wombat* books in the library so I was kind of published. I guess you could say I was an add-on author at age 8. It is the earliest experience of creativity I can remember.

At that age, creativity and imagination come naturally. As a child there are no dreams or expectations in front of you – only the expression of your imagination in the moment. If someone asks you to create, you create. You never stop to ask if it's possible or if you're any good – you just do it. Sadly, however, that changes as you get older.

High School Creativity

After Elementary school and all its freedom, High School happened. To be honest, it wasn't a great experience creatively. At times it felt like the system was trying to beat the imagination out of me, rather than foster it.

I got into trouble because I still thought that creativity would be welcome. It turns out I was very wrong. Remembering facts was welcome. Regurgitating whatever the teacher told you was welcome. Innovation and imagination were viewed as dissention and stamped out.

For example, I was scoring low on my English essays because I would answer the questions creatively. I was getting E and F grades. Finally we had this lunch time class for all the English dropouts. This guy said, *okay here's how you have to write your essays,* and he gave us the form and structure to use. It was very specific and ordered. There was no room for anything that diverged from the format. Once I gave up my creative ideas and adhered to that structure, I aced English and became a straight A student. Sound familiar?

It was about mimicking the precise form and structure that the English teaching system set. I don't blame the teacher – he was under orders! He was teaching me how to get good grades. Unfortunately, he had to train the wild random imaginative nature out of me to get them. He trained me to simply remember and repeat the answers he dictated to us and when I did, I was rewarded.

And I have to tell you, while I enjoyed mastering the system, writing those essays was *torture.*

College Creativity

Long story short, my creativity was beaten out of me by a system that was most interested in regurgitating facts and figures. Can you relate? A lot of the current education systems are set up that way. The only exceptions seem to be in softer subjects like art and music and even they get highly technical in the final high school years.

When I went to college, however, all that changed when someone invited me to a *college revue*. So what is a college revue? These shows are kind of like a live stage version of *Saturday Night Live*. Three or four hundred of us went into a college auditorium to be entertained. It had nothing do with teachers and lecturers. There was no form, no structure and no format. It was all students who prepared these amazing shows. This amazing variety show was performed by med students, law students, and the students of every discipline who cared to put one on. The teaching staff weren't involved at all. In short, these revues represented total creative freedom. At last!

In these college revues there would be comedy sketches, there would be voiceovers between the sketches as they reset the stage, there would be massive musical numbers with dozens of dancers, a ten piece band and lead singers. It was a real variety show, based on whatever was happening politically at the time and whatever larrikinism the kids were up to. By the way, larrikinism is an Australian term for mischief!

It was love at first sight.

I was just mesmerized! This was the funniest, most wonderful and creative performance I'd ever seen! I thought these people were the most glamorous, sexy and fantastic people I'd ever seen. So when I saw a little advertisement in the college newspaper calling for people to join in the next revue, I jumped at the chance. I joined the revue scene right away and was massively active for the next two or three years. I wound up doing all those things I'd seen on stage. I was the guy lead singing with the band. I danced, did a lot of character work, a lot of voice-over comedy work, a lot of live character work and then I wound up writing the sketches and finally directing my own show.

Just FYI, I directed the Medical Faculty review in 1994 with Lindy Elder. We called the show 'All the President's Phlegm'. Hey - I never said we were classy!

I think this was one of the most spectacularly creative things in my early life. The sky was the limit. We could lampoon anything! We did a scene with this stuff called Wizz Fizz, based on a children's white candy powder which was a kind of sherbert. In this wildly lateral scene, the premise was that the Wizz Fizz was actually cocaine. Kids were dealing but they were dealing sherbert! Then there was a scene about special effects where there was a chemist going to a CVS or Walgreens store but instead of selling drugs and pharmaceuticals they sold special effects sounds, so you would come in and say, "I was wondering if you had a little *Take me to the bridge?*" That's a line from a James Brown song I used to love.

I did a lot of really creative work on stage, writing, directing and performing. I was, in hindsight, retraining myself to be truly creative in the moment. I guess you could even say it led to this book!

Commercial Creativity

Of course after my education was over, I was keen to convert my learning into something that paid the rent. As many artists do, I tried my hand at many different creative forms of over the next decade or two. From writing scripts to recording CDs, from television shows to screenplays I've tried them all. Before I was able to truly express my creativity, however, I needed to learn how to work within the lines.

With that in mind, I began my creative career as many do, in a bleak grey cubicle within the world of big business.

My Scripts

I began by working for a corporate communications company in Sydney, Australia. There we crafted PowerPoint presentations, slideshows and speeches for the heads of industry. From the telecommunications industry to soup companies, from cat food to cell phones I worked with them all. I found myself working on web sites, videos and presentations for well-known brands like Whisker's cat food, Sony, Campbell's soup and IBM.

I started as an assistant, then a designer and programmer, then an art director and creative director. I was able to combine right brain creative skills with operational left brain skills. In other words, we delivered *results* not just ideas.

Over time, however, I got more and more frustrated working within the corporate world. It was creative only within limits, like, "Let's do comedy ... as long as it's about the new Dell laptop" or "Let's do a website ... as long as it's within the 3Com template." Or "Let's do some television ... as decided by the producers at Channel Seven."

Long story short, it didn't feel like *creative freedom*. I began to lust for a world without boundaries in which I could write, sing, shoot or produce absolutely anything I wanted. I began to moonlight writing album under the now embarrassing name of *Grooveboy*.

My Albums

While my work as Grooveboy was creatively satisfying, it never gained traction. It was probably because I never really performed live, preferring to stay within the comfortable borders of my bedroom home studio. Instead, my first commercially successful CDs and cassette tapes were a series of children's stories and games called *Carkids*.

I remember, in hindsight, I spent a lot of time just walking on the beach, talking with my brother who's a great friend and has great energy, and getting into that clear creative space. And then I sat down and this story just sort of flowed out of me. I jumped into production, recorded the voices, sound effects and soundtrack, made it all into CDs and sold over 10,000 copies. The first series of four titles cleared me about $80,000 profit over those first two years. It was a fantastic creative experience where I got to realize my creativity was valuable in a really hands-on grounded way. It could convert to actual cash in the bank. That was a real turning point for me.

My Books

After doing the CDs, I became very active in the children's book industry. I wrote a series of children's books, which were picked up and published by Random House. I've subsequently written more books that I've published around the world. I'm now in a new partnership with Simon and Schuster and Beyond Word, the imprint that created *The Secret*. We're in the midst of a project that we're hoping will introduce a new genre to children's writing called *empowerment fiction*.

My Carkids CDs were ultimately picked up by the Australian Broadcasting Commission.

My TV Show

After the books and albums did so well, I went live on stage for a year or so. We boiled down the best of the live work into a TV pilot which was picked up by a cable channel. The second season was picked up by Channel 9, the largest national broadcast network in Australia. It's kind of like CBS or NBC here in America.

In the end I did three seasons both as a producer and as the on-camera talent. I would go to sleep at night, dream up an episode, then get up the next day and brief my team. We did everything from creating rock-stars to pirate ship captains as the seasons unfolded.

Each show was an exercise in creativity as we entertained a national audience.

Go to http://www.timlevy.net/gdtv to see for yourself, or scan this QR code.

Strategic Creativity

I also began to explore creativity and innovation in a more strategic business sense. It has become a passion over the course of time, although it barely resembles those first stories in the back of *The Muddle Headed Wombat*!

These days I help people, especially CEOs and entrepreneurs, to find clarity and purpose in their lives. This turns out to be an extraordinarily diverse and creative exercise. We ask 'What would be a perfect life for you?', and then design the strategy to make it happen. Next, I work over time to guide the realization of these strategies as they emerge naturally in the real world.

I do the same work within medium sized businesses. It turns out that creative and innovative strategies are the key to rapid growth and profitability, as you'll already know if you've spent any time at my web site.

Go to http://www.timlevy.net or scan this QR code.

It's in the corporate arena that I've honed my skills working with CEOs and entrepreneurs day to day to bring their visions out of their minds and into reality.

My creative story, then is a balance of left and right brain. It's books, it's albums, it's DVDs, it's CDs, it's stage shows and it's TV. It's strategy, clarity and mind-set as I work with CEOs, entrepreneurs and creative people of all kinds.

This book, then, is a practical instructional guide. It is designed to take you through the concepts, tools and processes that I use day in a day out in my own creative practice. It is the sequence that has empowered me write all of those books, albums, TV shows and innovate business strategies.

I trust that these techniques will do the same for you.

CREATIVITY IN THE REAL WORLD

Creativity and Innovation

MR. JONES KNEW BILLY'S TENDENCY TO
TELL WILD STORIES WITH ABSOLUTE CONVICTION
WOULD MEAN AS AN ADULT HE'D
ONLY EVER BE ABLE TO WORK IN POLITICS.

Creativity in the Real World

Who Is This Book For?

So, who is the optimum audience for this book? I think it's easier to say who it's *not* for. The only people this book is *not* for (and to be fair this is a large group) are those who *are* not and *do not want to be* creative. A very left brain organization like the government, for example the DMV, might not find it useful. At the DMV you have to follow the guidelines, structures and practices perfectly or your boss will get very distressed. Even so - let's say if you're in that field: this book could be for your *after-hours* projects.

For example, I have a team member who is a video editor, and tremendously creative, but he works in a government legal department by day. In his day job he is involved in a very rigorous left brained task which simply primes him to be creative after-hours. Didn't Einstein work by day as a clerk in a patenting office? Someone who works within the rules by day might be looking to change the world through their art at night.

This book, then, is for everyone who wants to access and optimize their creativity. It's for everyone who wants to *untrain* themselves from the constriction of their education and *retrain* themselves into more optimal patterns.

- If you're a **CEO** or **entrepreneur**, this book is essential.

- If you're in **design, R&D**, or **programming** then this is perfect for you in your professional life.

- If you're an **artist**, a **writer** or **musician**, this book will help you access your inner muse.

- If you're interested in being creative as a **parent, caretaker** or **health professional**, then this book will bring new creativity to your relationship and day.

- And the list goes on!

Whether this is for work or play or anything in between, *this book is for everyone who wants to access their true creative genius and apply it in their lives.*

Creativity for CEOs and Entrepreneurs

I speak on clarity, strategy and creativity all around the world. Right now I'm focusing on CEO groups like Vistage, CEOSpace and Secret Knock. In these presentations, I poll the room, asking, "What is the most import thing that you, as a CEO and entrepreneur, spend your time doing?"

It always comes back to **creativity**. They might call it innovation, or they might call it vision, but it's always about creativity.

If you look at the most successful CEOs in recent times, Steve Jobs is a terrific example. When you look at what he's remembered for, it's not for his operational role in manufacturing, or efficiencies at the conveyor belt. He's remembered for absolutely revolutionizing five industries: music, film, iTunes, iPod, the tablet industry with the iPad. Tablets had come out before (for example, Microsoft had a tablet they envisioned for nurses in 2001 or 2002) but something about Jobs' imagination and creativity made that thing work.

There is some strange magic, some confluence of events and when that sort of gold happens, companies change, profit changes and the world changes. So creativity is staggeringly important for CEOs and they know it. When I say CEOs of course, I'm talking about all leaders and entrepreneurs also.

Creativity and New Income Streams

This is a key question. It brings to mind a call I had recently. I'm working with a CEO involved in industrial manufacturing. His business does well, turning over twenty-seven million annually, but in the last four months business has been slow. During our conversation he told me how his business is becoming commoditized and margins are shrinking. Instead of making 10 cents on the dollar he is making 5 cents and they're feeling squeezed. He feels they have to reduce expenses and overheads so as not to make a loss. He's looking into laying some people off to cope with this change in the market.

I wanted to think creatively before we made those moves.

"Let's consider some new income streams." I said, "Maybe we can explore some new markets and opportunities, expanding in other ways." He agreed and we started exploring options beyond his solution of a shrunken world.

Once we were in this more positive energetic state, we brought out focus to the emerging world of 3D printing. This technology is revolutionizing the manufacture of all physical products as you read these very words. We started looking at the edge: where is the energy there? Well, it turns out there's an event called the Maker Fair in San Francisco in May. We're considering going there together with no agenda beyond just walking around and seeing what cool creative ideas, connections, people and businesses show up. In this way, we are taking a contraction and beginning to make it into an expansion.

This creative and lateral idea suddenly breathed new life in to this guy. He was suddenly full of enthusiasm and passion. As quickly as that, the energy shifted and we started seeing options.

By the end of the call we had identified four separate new income streams for his business. While these four new experiments might take a little while to bring profit to the company, they're steering it towards growth right now.

A New Way to Sell Coffee

I've got another cool story: this time about a marketing executive. I was speaking on creativity and innovation to a group of CMOs, chief marketing officers, and I remember one who ran a big coffee business. The thing about coffee is, it's been sold for a long time and there are only so many ways to sell it. The picture of the person drinking that first sip in the morning: the beautiful looking cup of coffee: there are only so many ways to think about it, shoot it or pitch it. The CMO was complaining that his team had run out of new ideas. He was even beginning to think that there were no original ways to sell coffee left at all!

What we were able to do was really cool. Using one of the tools we will get to later in this book, we accessed a creative community of artists. We were able to browse a catalogue of *over 25 million different pieces of artwork* in real time. We browsed different interpretations of morning ritual coffee, waking up, all sorts of things. Ideas started to flow and within minutes we had a brand new campaign for that company.

You could feel the energy in the room shift. We went, as a group, from distressed and contracted to awake, alive and passionate in moments.

And when we did, this CMO suddenly accessed his creativity again. Within minutes, we had a slew of new ideas to bring to the table. Of course in the end, that becomes the pattern interrupt which becomes new sales for that brand of coffee and obviously has a financial impact in the end. You should have just seen this guy light up! There's something about creativity and the process of creating that is essentially human and wildly fulfilling. It's just part of being alive. People feel better when they're creating.

Creativity for Artists

The biggest group of people visibly involved in creativity includes any kind of artist, sculptor, singer, dancer, writer, actor or musician.

Jazz musicians are a great example of that. I've had the great fortune to be active in a lot of these creative roles. I spent three years doing improv jazz with the Sydney Dance Company School and doing comedy improv on stage. You need your creativity there from moment to moment. So whether it's in art, personal life, or business this creativity is critical for everybody.

If jazz musicians want to move up into the higher ranks of their specific field, with higher pay, they have to be leaders and innovators. If you listen to a jazz musician and you feel you've heard it before, you feel it's not as good as the one who's creating something innovative and new. If you watch a movie and feel that, even though the actors are different, you've seen that story before or you can predict the ending, then it's not a great movie. It's the movie with a twist that gets your attention: it's the story with the unanticipated jab or move or ending that is fantastic or fulfilling. The truth is humans love to be surprised in that way, and that's where creativity and innovation come in.

Waking Up Your Creativity

Of course, sometimes it's not easy to jump into a creative mode. It can be especially difficult if you haven't used it in a while. Your imagination can get rusty!

Reawakening the creative muscle can be much the same as training physical muscles in the gym for the first time in years. The result can be stiffness and pain in the morning. Have you ever had a stiff and painful brain? It happens.

One time, when I was speaking, I had one poor guy who just couldn't handle it – and he got so upset! Everyone else was drawing, using colorful pens and markers. They were mind mapping and drawing pictures. They were full of energy, alive and animated. Everyone was having a great time – except one guy. This one guy was looking around the room, seeing what he was missing out on and getting mad. He held his peace until the very end of this three or four hour workshop. At the very end when people started giving their opinion he stood up and started yelling at me!

I think it had just been too long since he'd used his creative muscle and the whole thing was too much for him. That's only happened to me once, because 99.9% of the time people just love it. When they are being creative, they just engaged, alive and glowing.

Peanuts and Poetry

Here's a beautiful story. One guy I remember was on my left hand side at the front of the audience. He said, "Listen, the thing that happens to me is this. When I am on a plane I get those little napkins that come with the peanuts and *I write poetry on the napkins.*"

I said, "What do you mean?" and he said, "Well it's the only place I feel like doing that. It just comes out of me, and I write poetry on the napkins and I ball it up and put them away and I don't show anyone."

"Don't you even show your wife or your kids?" I asked.

"No. It's my little secret."

This guy was obviously a *true poet* but he felt the world around him wasn't ready for his poetry. Despite everything it still leaked out of him.

I see that happening all the time. Most people are so intrinsically creative that if they don't express themselves, it begins to happen anyway. At some level, the song wants to be sung, the book wants to be written, the characters want to come alive, and the painting and the drawings come out as doodles. When you're in school teachers say, "Stop doodling. Stop daydreaming," when really that creativity just wants to come out. For me this is the stuff that changes the world.

Reconnecting With Your Childhood Imagination

I believe most people absolutely want to reconnect with their childhood imagination and creativity. The great gift in my life is I get to be the guy who goes and puts people into that creative space. I get these really stodgy "I've got a company that has 1600 trucks in the fleet" businessmen, and have them act like kids. I used to feed them candy just to get them back to their childhood and have them really come alive creatively!

Now, I use a set of specific tools and processes to get them there. Let's jump into Section Two where I'll introduce those tools and have you configure them for your own life through a series of quick, fun and engaging exercises. Get your pens ready!

SECTION TWO

Creativity and Innovation

Section Two

Aspect Overview

This chapter is where the rubber really meets the road. This is where we explore the concepts, tools and processes you'll need to optimize your creativity and innovation. There are six aspects to this practice.

1. The first aspect is **creativity math**. This is the underlining logic and math that lives beneath this entire book. This is the single conceptual equation that makes it all make sense.

2. The second aspect is concept of **the energy spectrum.** We explore the spectrum of energy from high to low and its connection to your levels of clarity, creativity and innovation.

3. The third aspect is **energy management tools.** We'll go through six groups of tools and the exercises that you can do to personalize them.

4. The fourth aspect is **mind soup**. This is about an analogy, a funny story about cans of soup! It explains the importance of an empty mind for your innovation and creativity, and how to fix problems that can come up.

5. The fifth aspect is **the creativity practice.** This is about understanding how your brain works, in particular the two sides of your brain, left and right, and the sequence in which they can best work together.

6. The sixth aspect is **external creativity**. In the event your *own* creativity and innovation fail to provide you answers, what external resources can you access to get the creativity and innovation you need?

Aspect # 1

THE CREATIVITY MATH

Creativity and Innovation

DAVE'S ADVANCED

ENERGY CONSERVATION POLICY

AT WORK.

Aspect #1 - The Creativity Math

Over the course of time I started to realize that there is an essential connection between the level of energy and the level of creativity you have. Simply put, as a mathematical equation,

Energy = Creativity

This means when your energy is very high, you're creative, clear and in an optimum state. When your energy is very low, you're foggy, unoriginal and generally brain-dead. Simple, right?

Most people can intuitively relate to this. When you're feeling down, everything seems bleak and dark and it's hard to come up with new ideas. When you're strolling happily along a beach, your mind empty, happy and free then ideas tend to drop right in!

So as my energy goes up, my clarity goes up and my creativity goes up also. As my energy goes down my clarity goes down and I just can't see things. I get foggy. I get lost. As I started to explore this with other people I realized it was part of the human condition for everybody.

It's logical when you think about it this way. The math makes it super clear.

But Wait, There's More!

Of course, most people want to raise their energy. As we said, when you're at that higher end of the spectrum, you get all of the benefits – innovation, creativity, and not just those. Here are some further benefits of attaining and maintaining a high energy state:

- Increased clarity

- Deeper and more connected relationships

- Deeper alignment to your purpose and passion in life

- Along with deeper relationships comes higher levels of

intimacy and physical connection

- physical benefits including vitality and kinetic energy

- Finally, since energy and money are also closely related you'll find higher energy = higher money, too.

For more information check out http://www.timlevy.net/money or just scan this QR code.

So the question becomes how can I manage my energy to be in a high energy state? In other words, how can I give myself the best possible chance to access my true creative genius by moving to a high energy state?

You're in luck. This section of the book is about doing just that. I'm about to give you the tools and processes to get to your own best high energy state and stay there.

Making It Personal

The interesting thing is that the triggers to high energy and low energy states can be *different for everyone.*

For example, let's consider horror movies. You know the ones

- Saw I and Saw II and ... how many of those are there? The point is that some people *love* those movies. They show up, pay their money and have a terrific time. Their heart pounds, their blood rushes and their soul is tickled in a positive way. They leave the theater in a high energy state.

And then, there's me. I just cannot stand horror movies. You cannot force me to watch them because I know that there's nothing there for me. I hate the blood, I hate the guts and hate the constant state of fear and violence. Even the *thought* of a horror movie experience triggers a bad feeling inside me, lowering my energy. It's happening now even as I write about it – quick – let's move on!

So managing your own energy is all about finding your own personal triggers. In the next section, we'll go through six specific toolsets and the accompanying exercises designed to bring out your own, personal configurations.

Your Best Shot

Of course, at the end of the day, you cannot force creativity. In fact, if you look into the typical artist's journey of creativity, you'll find a whole mythology about this. It's the Greek mythology about *the muse*. The Muses are, according to the story, non-physical Goddesses of creativity. There's one for literature, one for science and one for the arts.

The idea is that as you're hoping to create something, the relevant muse will visit your mind and place a great idea there. They call it connecting to your muse or maybe in today's terminology your *inner voice*.

However you conceive of it, everyone agrees that while you cannot force great ideas, great stories and concepts, you can *encourage them*. You can consciously create the most conducive or optimal environment for creativity and innovation to arise.

That's what this book is all about. It's about creating the best possible high energy environment for you, giving you your *best shot* at creativity.

A Quick Mental Exercise

Let's do a quick mental exercise to illustrate this.

Imagine a time when you were unhappy. Maybe you were in tears, maybe you were depressed, or something bad had happened. It got you into that sort of fog, that stuck place. Is it easy to dig yourself out of depression? It's almost impossible. You don't have great ideas, innovation, creativity, good answers, new techniques or technology when you're in a very low energetic state.

Now, consider a time when you were feeling terrific! That feels much nicer, right? Focus, in your mind, on a time where everything was going beautifully. Imagine a time when you were doing something wonderful, something fun and engaging. Bring those feelings of happiness back into your mind, body and soul.

At this point, you'll naturally be in a higher energetic state. Even the simple act of visualization is a powerful tool, here. And when you're feeling charged and energized, then your creativity flows easily. Innovation comes to you effortlessly, easily and your state is optimum for all things creative.

There's a lesson here. If I have a pressing problem, rather than getting stressed or upset, I focus on raising my energy up to the highest possible level.

One neat trick I do is to go to a local supermarket called Whole Foods. There are Whole Foods stores all across America, and one of the things some of the larger venues share is that they have a full-time massage team. Seriously.

I go into Whole Foods and get myself a massage, generally for 15 or 30 minutes at a time. It's very inexpensive, maybe $15 - 30 plus a tip. From the moment the masseur puts their hands on me, I can feel wonderful energy pouring into my body. I can feel the warmth of their hands, the kinetic energy of the movement as well as the energy of their focus and intention. All of that charges me up and suddenly I feel terrific again. That's when the ideas flow. I'll sit there allowing a particular issue to run through my mind as I'm being massaged. And when I do, creative solutions flow effortlessly into my mind pretty much every time. And if they don't – well that's what more massage is for, right?!

While the triggers that get you into a particular energetic state are different for everybody, the common thread is that when your energy is high, you have great creativity, and when your energy is low you don't. Simple as that.

Aspect #2

THE ENERGY
SPECTRUM

Creativity and Innovation

EINSTEIN'S LESSER KNOWN

ENERGY EQUATION.

Aspect #2 – The Energy Spectrum

Let's move onto the next topic, the central concept of a *spectrum of energy*.

The energetic spectrum is a conceptual continuum of personal energetic states. You can use this concept to assess your personal energetic state or level at any one moment.

I like to visualise the energetic spectrum as a kind of *energetic thermometer* that ranges from plus ten to minus ten. At the top of the thermometer is 10 out of 10 energy, when you're just as energized as you can be. At 0 you're kind of neutral, and at -10 you're at the lowest you can be. Let's talk about those different energetic states, starting from the very, very top.

The Top of the Spectrum

It's a wonderful thing to be at the top of the energetic spectrum. When your energy level is at positive 10, you're feeling as wonderful as a human can possibly feel.

To be honest, I don't think most people ever get there, but when you get to this point, it's what **awake** looks like. That's what **enlightened** looks like. This is the energetic state Buddha was in when finding enlightenment under the tree.

This was quite a revelation for me. I realize now that when you're at this kind of level, the world is a very different place. It's flowing, easy, effortless and fun.

It's at a positive 10 energetic level that extraordinary connection to the muse or spirit or the universe or God, depending on how you see spirituality, lives. At this level creativity and creative genius are just effortless, almost like you can access some kind of collective consciousness directly. There, great ideas and great thoughts flow easily and effortlessly to you.

The High Reaches of the Spectrum

Let's come down to a plus 5 energetic state. The way I see this spectrum, this is where most people want to be, where most people max out. Being at positive 5 is the best possible moment on an already amazing day.

For example, when we moved from Australia to America we flew across the International Date Line on Christmas day. We got up on Christmas day in Sydney, then had a *second* Christmas day in Los Angeles! During the first Christmas day, my children especially were already on an energetic high. They were probably at a positive 2 from simple excitement. It's Christmas! Then, after they got a bunch of presents, they were even more alive at perhaps a positive 3. Then we jumped on a jumbo jet and woke up to a *second* Christmas day at *Disneyland!* The children nearly exploded with job, which left them at a positive 5.

For me, it can be a simple as sitting in that massage chair at Whole Foods. Aaah. Delicious. Maybe it's just an intimate dinner with my wife and a few foods friends. I'm at a definite positive 5 when I'm on stage, performing to a group of 500 or 1,000 joyous humans. Although I understand that's not true for everyone!

And when you're really high energy, innovation, clarity and creativity are easy. This is where writer's flow lives. What's writer's flow? It's the opposite of the dreaded writer's block. This is that great high energy place.

The Middle of the Spectrum

Being at zero in this spectrum is kind of neutral. This is when you're sort of living your life half asleep. You're going through the motions. You have just enough energy to drag yourself out of bed, into your commute, to your job, which you probably don't love, and through the end of the day trying to make sure your boss doesn't scream at you too much. Then you drag yourself home, done for the day, to scrape together some food, possibly not great food because you don't have the energy to cook something fantastic, then go to bed. You wake up the next morning and it's like Groundhog Day. Your life feels like it's on repeat. Finally, Friday afternoon comes and there's a sense of freedom. Thank Goodness it's Friday, right? However, you wind up using the weekend to get your energy back after your draining week. And now you're ready to start again.

That kind of half-asleep mode is what I call an energetic state of zero, neutral. Thoughts and creativity and innovation are sporadic here, which is why I think it's hard to be wildly entrepreneurial starting from that place.

The Lower Reaches of the Spectrum

Of course the spectrum doesn't end there. Lower energy, -3, -5, we talk about as sadness, anxiety and eventually, **depression**. Of course there might be medical, chemical, or genetic reasons, but also some people just get deeply unhappy. They're depressed and living in pain. This might be a physical thing. My wife doesn't have an awesome relationship with the dentist, so she's just deeply unhappy when she's told her teeth need some fillings! And it's even worse when she's in the dentist' chair.

There are things that leave you in pain and distressed and unhappy: divorce, depression, long- term physical illness, all those sorts of things. And when you're in that depressed place, it's like you're stuck in a hole and you just can't see the way out. It's like the world is somehow darker and lacking hope.

At this end of the spectrum, it's almost impossible to dig yourself out of the hole. Your access to creativity and innovation is almost nil. If you think you're here, it would be wise to get some skilled counselling, talk to a therapist, or talk to your doctor. And of course, use the toolsets we're about to introduce and configure to lift your energetic state.

The Bottom of the Spectrum

At the very bottom of this spectrum is negative 10. That's when you're in so much pain you start thinking that life is just not worth living. At a negative 10 it can feel like it would be less painful to just check out. It's very difficult to think clearly at all at this point. That's why most societies set up a depression hot line, putting someone with better energy a simple phone call away. If you think you're here, seek professional help *immediately*.

Working with the Spectrum

So, there's your spectrum from negative 10 all the way up to positive 10.

And how do you work with this knowledge?

Clearly you want to manage yourself to be somewhere between 0 and 5, at 2, 3, 4 and 5 as much as possible.

- That's when you're happy, high energy, well charged, innovative and creative,

- That's where you can see your way out of any tricky situation and see your way into any situation you want to get into.

- That's is where great vision and reason live,

- That' where entrepreneurs live, where good business ideas come from, where new income streams live.

- That's where creativity in the forms of stories, songs, artwork and sculpture live.

- That's where terrific and deep connections and relationships live,

All those things live up there in that positive 3, 4 or 5 part of the spectrum, way above that 0 level. That's what the energy spectrum is about, and that's where you want to be. And everybody wants to have the benefits that live up there – creativity, innovation, terrific connection and relationships, and many more.

It's that top half of the energy spectrum that is your optimal state for creativity and innovation.

So. Now that we know what the spectrum looks like, let's look at how to get into this state and stay there.

Aspect #3

ENERGY TOOLSETS

Creativity and Innovation

WE CAN'T AFFORD A RETREAT AND
A SWEAT LODGE, SO I'VE JUST TURNED
THE AIR CONDITIONING OFF.

Aspect #3 - Energy Toolsets

Now that you're aware of the connection between energy and creativity, the key question is '*How do I manage my energy level?*' More importantly, "*How do I boost my level to 5 or above?*"

The following sections detail 7 different toolsets that you can use to manage your energy up or down – the choice is yours!

1. **Fuel** – What you put into your body

2. **Movement** – How you move your body

3. **Location** – The connection between energy and place

4. **People** – The energy of the people you hang out with

5. **Sound and Color** – What you put into your ears

6. **Ritual** – Your personal energy raising sequences, and

7. **Things to Avoid** – The energetic toxins in your life.

With each toolset, I'll give you loads of examples as well as an exercise designed to help you personalize it. Most people find five or ten individual tools for each area we examine through the exercises. That way you'll finish this book with a slew of tools to manage your personal energy, each configured for your individual life.

And why do I call these 7 focus areas *toolsets?* Let me explain. When you do each exercise, you're going to identify a series of answers to each question. For example, you might identify protein bars, walnuts and cashew nuts as **foods** that raise your energy and all Jamba Juices as **drinks** that do the same. Now you have four tools – protein bars, walnuts, cashew nuts and Jamba Juices – in your energy raising toolkit. If you want to raise your energy simply deploy your tools and hey presto! You'll raise your energy. Easy, right?

Before We Begin

For this to happen, you need to get 7 pieces of paper and something to write with. Blank paper would be ideal, although you can have lined paper if you wish. The writing implements might be colorful markers, crayons, colored pencils, or might just be a straight old black pen. Either way, we're going to answer 7 questions dealing with the 7 different toolsets.

Toolset One - Fuel

Let's start with energy toolset number one, **fuel**. What do I mean by fuel? One of the biggest things you can do to influence your personal energy is to look at what you eat.

What's the fuel you put in your body? Simply put, some foods and drinks make you feel great, and some make you feel terrible.

Have you ever come to the end of a meal and thought to yourself *'Man, I feel sleepy. I gotta have a nap!'* Feeling tired is, obviously, a low energy state. Logic says that what you just ate put you into a food coma. It's low energy food for you. So it's not the ideal food to eat *just before* you go into a high-level business brainstorm. Unless, of course, you're hoping to sleep through it. It happens, right?

If you look at food, you probably know which things are low

energy for you – they're the ones that make you feel sleepy, grumpy or irritable. They're things that are tough to digest and make your stomach feel bad.

Often these are the kinds of highly-processed foods that you'll find in the snack isle at the supermarket. These include all the standard party favorites like candy, chips and cola. Are you beginning to see a pattern?

Fried chips and burgers, probably for most people, are on the lower end of the energy spectrum. High sugar products might give you a burst for a while, but when the sugar crash hits it leaves you stranded in a low energetic state. We're looking for things that are good for your energy *long term*. This means you're more likely to focus on proteins, for example, which give energy over longer periods of time and rarely leave you crashed or depleted.

Things I look for when it comes to good energy – and I've worked with enough people over time to believe these are common – are things like fresh fruit, fresh vegetables, and freshly cooked foods, as opposed to wildly pre-packaged, pre-processed and irradiated foods that line the shelves of most standard supermarkets. In Texas, that means focusing on supermarkets like Whole Foods and Central. And as a general rule, organic foods will have a higher energy than their conventional counterparts.

My favorite food, for example, is a bowl of organic cherries – fantastic. Fruits and vegetables, particularly green vegetables, seem to be good. Raw foods seem to be good. Those are some guidelines.

Super Conscious Road Warrior

Imagine you have a special set of foods that put you into a great, high-vitality and high-energy state just before you go into a creative session? Would that increase your chances of success?

My amazing food consultant Artemis designed something he calls 'Super-conscious road warrior' which I take with me when I travel. I grab a drink of it *just before* I go on stage to speak and hey presto! It's amazing. I've found that I'm much more likely to have a great talk and get loads of laughter and interaction with my audience when I drink this stuff.

High Energy Food

My current favorite foods are called *super foods*. Seriously, it's a technical term. These are things like spirulina that you get in crazy powder containers over at Whole Foods. Go into Whole Foods or find a good naturopath who can help you with real expertise here, and ask them about high alkaline super foods.

High Energy Water

One of the things that is really important at my house is a good drink. A lot of drink is not awesome. Soda and highly sugared beverages are not great energy food. Even the normal water that comes out of a tap may not be awesome. We get all our water in a big five-gallon drum from Whole Foods. If you want to spend a bit more money, you can buy water from the supermarket or get one of the purifiers that does highly alkaline water. I also like the Fiji water, although it's expensive.

Those are some of the things I do to keep my energy up in terms of good fuel. Some of the side benefits are that obviously I've got good energy for moving around, kinetic energy, athletic energy, and also it keeps my weight down which is a side benefit too. Either way, it gets your energy up, which is what's important.

Exercise One – Your High Energy Fuels

What I'd like you to do is this: put down this book for a moment. Write the words 'My High Energy Fuels' at the top of the page, and then answer these questions –

What foods and drinks _raise my energy?_

What foods and drinks _lower my energy?_

What are your personal answers to these questions? I've given you loads of examples, so take 60 seconds and give me 5 or 10 answers to each question on that first piece of paper.

Toolset Two – Movement

The next toolset is *physical movement.* As you know the mind and body are s t r o n g l y interconnected, sometimes even referred to in one breath as the *body-mind.* What this means is that when something happens in the body, it immediately effects the mind. When something happens in the mind, it effects the body.

For example, trainers often have their athletes rehearse a race in their mind before the race is actually run and when they do, the body responds in real-time as if the race was *actually being run.* The heart rate increases and the adrenal glands begin to fire. Visualisation, which we'll refer to again later, is a powerful energetic technique.

This is why physical movement is so effective in raising your energy. For example, if you simply jump up, turn on your favorite music and start to dance, you'll raise your energy. I frequently do this when I speak to get the energy of the room up before I begin. Conversely, if you lower the lights, put in ear-plugs and lie down on a bed, you'll lower your energy as your body takes the cue to move into a sleep state.

What I like to do is simply go for a walk around my neighbourhood. I take one of my children with me and we do a half-hour lap. Another thing we love to do, when we're on holiday, is swim. We especially like jumping in and out of a pool – as you can see in the image above. That's our older son Zak at play. The physical movement raises the energy in my body and hence, because of the connection, my mind. My children have a favorite movement: dance. Our younger son Finn is an avid tap dancer. He *always* comes back from his dance class with his energy high, as does my daughter Bell. Zak loves his gymnastics class which always leaves him happy and excited. We also run a regular disco in our living room, care of Pandora.com.

Exercise Two – Your High Energy Movements

OK. Please put down the book and grab your next page. Write the words 'My High Energy Movements' at the top of the page, and then answer these questions –

What physical movements _raise my energy?_

What physical movements _lower my energy?_

What are your personal answers to this question? I've given you loads of examples, so take 60 seconds and give me 5 or 10 answers to each question on that _second_ piece of paper.

Toolset Three - Location

The next toolset is **location** or **place**. Simply put, some places have better energy than others. Let me explain.

I happen to love being *near* the water, and being *in* the water is even better. In fact, I'm automatically happy when I'm in a beautiful, outdoor, natural place. Anytime I'm walking along a beach in Sydney, or maybe on the coast somewhere in California or Florida, I naturally fall into a high energy state.

One particular example is a place north of San Francisco called the Harbin Hot Springs. It's an absolutely beautiful property. A few decades ago, some innovative and visionary people bought this property and harnessed the natural waters that come from miles underneath the ground. If you visit, you can soak in beautiful pools that have been crafted by artisans. You can just linger in the sunshine, in hot or cold water or simply on a beautiful timber deck under the trees. The energy of the place is just fantastic. They have seriously high energy food there, too. The place draws very relaxed and happy people, a reasonably strong alternative crowd, lots of artists and creatives, dancers, yoga aficionados and just good vibes. For me it's a high energy place.

Another high energy example is the Baha'i Temple in Sydney. My family is highly *spiritual* so it's a good place for all of us. There's something *sacred* about a place steeped in tradition where people have been praying for hundreds of years. Somehow these areas seem to accumulate a fantastic energy.

The same is true for really amazing outdoor places, like Yosemite National Park in California. These natural places, with old redwood trees for example, have an amazing natural energy.

The opposite is also true. For example, if you have a job that you hate, when you get to that little gray cubicle and you're surrounded by symbols of things you don't like to do, that's probably a low energy place. Or if you go to a place where there was trauma or an accident to you, or your family, that's probably a low energy place. Graveyards, for example, are probably a low energy place for most people. Then again, people into horror movies and dead spirits probably love them! It's all about how each location *affects you*.

In that way there are high energy places and there are low energy places.

Location Awareness

When I work with CEOs, I love to take them somewhere high energy. I ask them, where is a really high energy place for you? And I've been to some fantastic places. Once I spent the day doing strategic creative work in a botanical garden. A different day I was up to my knees in the Narrabeen Lakes in Sydney. I've spent these CEO days hiking through the woods. I've spent them in places with great childhood memories, like the town of Hershey where chocolate is made in Pennsylvania.

In Austin, Texas, where I live, I've found a great place called The Writing Barn, run by my friend Bethany. Writers go there to write, take workshops and go on creative retreats. That's why I think the energy is so good! You get there and there's an old barn that used to have animals in it. It has a beautiful tin roof so you can hear the wind and rain, and a whole bunch of green and trees outside. It's not stuck in the middle of a city. Cities are high energy for some, but I like to retreat a little bit from that. The Writing Barn is certainly quiet as well.

Off-site creative places work so well in business because you get out of the low energy of the office and all of its phone calls and emails and get to somewhere that's just better energy. It makes you feel better and straight away your energy goes up and hence you have extra access to your creativity and innovation.

One favorite place of mine is the Pescadero Lighthouse in California, south of San Francisco. I have taken groups of people out there because when they get there, they just feel terrific. We were able to take an executive team and put them in this amazing hot tub that's hanging over the edge of the ocean. You see and hear the crashing waves and smell the saltwater and you just sit in the hot tub and chill out. Great ideas and deep connections happen effortlessly in that tub.

Exercise Three – Your High Energy Locations

OK. Please put down the book and grab your next page. Write the words 'My High Energy Locations' at the top of the page, and then answer these questions –

What locations _raise my energy_?

What locations _lower my energy_?

What are your personal answers to this question? I've given you loads of examples, so take 60 seconds and give me 5 or 10 answers to each question on that _third_ piece of paper.

A Few Notes

And here's a quick note. You might not have even been to some of the places you write down. That's OK. You might just feel the call. A high energy place for me would be Machu Picchu in South America, although I've never been there! Even though you've never been there, you just feel like you know these are high energy places for you.

And here's a further note. Make sure you list a couple in your **local area**, maybe a good restaurant or a good cinema, or a friend's house, or just a great place out in nature. List some high energy locations that are nearby as well as some that are **further away**.

Further Examples

I love the idea of having a spread of places that are easy and cheap to get to at the low end and places that are expensive and hard to get to at the high end.

For example right near where I live is something called *the green belt*. We can walk there in five minutes and it's a huge nature preserve. There is a place there my son calls *the stick place* because when we first went there we saw a massive pile of sticks. The stick place is a natural high energy outdoor location that's also free!

There is a seat that somebody painted and put out in the woods and I can go sit there and meditate or hang out. It's a good high energy place that's five minutes away and costs me nothing.

At the other end of the spectrum is Machu Picchu which is a long way away and would cost a bunch of money.

The point is that the location raises your energy. And being there or even just dreaming about being there has an effect on your energy level.

Toolset Four - People

The third energy toolset is **people**. In this model, let's says there are two kinds of people.

First, there are the people who raise your energy. Whether you spend five minutes or five hours or five days with them, you *just feel better*. You're in an energy surplus position. Let's call these **energy surplus** people.

Second, there are the people who drain your energy. Whether you spend two minutes, five minutes, an hour, or a day, you always wind up feeling *worse*. These are your **energy deficit** people.

Sometimes, you need to look no further than your own family to find your energy deficit people! This is why getting together on holidays can be a drain for some people. The problems happen when you're forced to be with people who, for you, are energy deficit people. It's no fun at all!

Just to be clear, this is no judgment on these people. They might be terrific with someone else, but with you, there's an energy deficit situation. You know who I'm talking about – this is the person who is always complaining, or who always triggers bad memories for you. Or maybe they always do something that's really annoying and which gets on your nerves. Or maybe they're always demanding and selfish. Whatever it is, in the end you just feel worse. These are good people to avoid, if you can.

The opposite are your energy surplus people. It doesn't seem to matter what you're doing with them, whether you go to a movie or you're washing the dishes together or doing a work project, you just always wind up feeling better. Maybe they're always making great jokes or maybe they're just really great listeners. Maybe they always have terrific ideas so it's easy and fun to work with them. Maybe they're diligent, maybe they work hard. Maybe they're lovely and generous. Maybe they're just great huggers! You know these people that every time you see them, they give you a big hug and you just feel better? Those are the energy surplus people.

The energy surplus people get you up, and the energy deficit people drag you down. It makes sense to spend time around high energy surplus people when you want to get your energy up with a view to doing something creative or innovative. And to be honest, you don't even have to meet with them in person. Just take a moment to call or text them for a sometimes lesser but still energetically positive boost.

Exercise Four – Your High Energy People

OK. Please put down the book again and grab your next page. Write the words 'My High Energy People' at the top of the page, and then answer these questions –

Who are my *energy surplus* people?

Who are my *energy deficit* people?

What are your personal answers to this question? I've given you loads of examples, so take 60 seconds and give me 5 or 10 answers to each question on that *fourth* piece of paper.

Toolset Five – Sound and Color

The fifth toolset is really underestimated in the world, and it's all about **sound** and **color**. What are the sounds that get your energy up, and what are the sounds that get your energy down? What are the colors that get your energy up, and what are the colors that get your energy down?

The effects of sounds on your concentration are well known. You would never try to write a book, for example, sitting next to someone working with a jackhammer. Would you never aim to relax and read the Sunday paper with a violent movie blasting away at top volume on the TV right next to you. You would turn the TV off, preferring peace and quiet as a backdrop to relaxation.

Equally, color has a role in your energetic state. Bright, prime colors bring energy where pale, gentler colors can drain it away.

If you visual red, surround yourself with red and wear red you'll know it's an energizing color. If you surround yourself with beige or even white, you'll know it's more peaceful.

The Importance of Sound

So what sounds get *your* energy up? It's different for everybody – some people like white noise, like the sound of the ocean, the tide coming in and out, the waves coming in and out over the sand, or maybe the wind in the trees or just other sounds of nature. For others, it's the sound of a baseball game or the super bowl.

For a lot of people, the number one energy management sound is *music*. What sort of music do you like? The funny thing is the same music can trigger a completely different reaction in two different people. For example, when I was young, I found classical music a real sedative; it just put me to sleep. It really brought my energy down. Now, I kind of love it. So I've changed over the course of time. What is the sort of music you like? Is it R&B, is it soul, is it hip-hop, is it metal? What is the music that gets your energy up?

The Importance of Color

Color is so important, incidentally, that is has an entire system dedicated to it in Eastern culture. The Indian culture has an entire science around energy and *chakras*. The seven chakras are energetic centres in your body, each represented by a color. Let's work from the bottom to the top.

- The 1st chakra is red, based at the tailbone

- The 2nd chakra is orange, based in the pelvis

- The 3rd chakra is yellow, based in the solar plexus

- The 4th chakra is green, based in the heart

- The 5th chakra is blue, based in the throat

- The 6th chakra is purple, based in the centre of the brow between the eyes

- The 7th chakra is violet, based at the crown of the head

There are thousands of years of history, research and practice here which I'll not attempt to summarize. At a basic level, the clear association is that if you surround yourself with red, you'll cause the base chakra to resonance, bringing more physical energy. You'll find violet better for meditation – and everything in between.

The salient facts here are that some colors energize and some deplete. The greys and beiges of work cubicles in a corporate environment, for example, rarely energize the workforce. Places like Google and Silicon Graphics before them have offices crammed with energizing reds, blues and greens.

In this way, color can be an effective energy management tool for you. If, for example, you're energized by purple, then you could surround your creative areas with purple. You could have purple pens, purple paper, purple screen-savers and purple feature walls. You might use more subdued colors in your bedroom to gently lower your energy in preparation for rest.

Exercise Five – Your High Energy Sounds and Colors

OK. Please put down the book and grab your next page. Write the words 'My High Energy Sounds and Colors' at the top of the page, and then answer these questions –

What kinds of sounds and colors *raise my energy*?

What kinds of sounds and colors *lower my energy*?

What are your personal answers to this question? I've given you loads of examples, so take 60 seconds and give me 5 or 10 answers to each question on that *fifth* piece of paper.

What are your top five or 10 pieces of music or sorts of sounds that bring your energy up? List a couple to make sure to avoid as well, that bring your energy down. All the good music, all the bad, all the good sound. Do the exercise. Jump in, now.

Toolset Six - Ritual

Here's the sixth toolset. It is a little hard to explain, but it's sort of the "everything else" category. I call it ritual. What are the things you do that are *uniquely you* that bring your energy up? Let me give you some examples from my life.

One of the things that brings my energy up is watching funny movies. I love, for example, the Mel Brooks DVD box set. I can watch them endlessly. And action movies aren't bad either, although I tend to prefer the ones that aren't full of blood and angst. Last night I watched the 2012 version of *The Three Musketeers*. It made my energy terrific. Stand-up comedy will get my energy up, too.

I have a new favourite ritual to kick start my day. I have an iPad with the Pandora app that plays endless music. Everyone knows about Pandora! What a lot of people don't know, however, is that it has a *comedy channel.* I play the comedy channel while I'm having a shower, brushing my teeth and getting ready in the morning. By the time I'm up, dressed and ready to face the day, I've been laughing for twenty minutes already. It's a great energy booster for me!

Other physical rituals like walking along the beach, or walking in nature raise my energy. Playing with my children is a huge one, too.

We have a little ritual at my house that we do every time we come and go. We love to hug each other and a little kiss doesn't hurt either. When my kids go off to school, we hug. When my kids come home from school, we hug. When I wake up and see my wife for the first time in the morning, we hug. When I get home from a meeting, we hug. Getting the picture? Each time there's a little exchange of energy that helps a little. The deeper and more connected the hug, the more energy happens for both of us. On the odd occasion we'll even gather up the whole family and squish in together.

So what are the rituals that get your energy up? I went through this exercise with a CEO and he said the thing he loved to do was get on his Harley and just go for a ride. It made him feel terrific and that was his ritual. Other people have a more physical ritual, like going to the gym, going for a long distance bike ride, or doing something else that sort of gets them out of their head and into their body. That's an important ritual for some. So what is your ritual? What is it that you uniquely do that gets your energy up? It might be on your own, or with someone else - maybe one of your energy surplus friends.

The Energy of Visualization

One powerful ritual is *visualization*. This is where you imagine something happen in your mind's eye. Some people do this as an actual visual picture, others hear and imaginary voice in their mind. Either way, simply put, the ritual here is to focus on a past or future experience in your mind. When you pick something positive, such as my children's Christmas day at Disneyland, the positive energy will flood back into you as if it's happening in the current moment! Of course, if you pick something upsetting, it will lower your energetic state. So the conscious practice of visualizing positive experiences is a great way to raise your energetic state.

Exercise Six – Your High Energy Sounds

OK. Please put down the book and grab your next page. Write the words 'My High Energy Rituals' at the top of the page, and then answer this question –

What are *my* high energy rituals?

What are your personal answers to this question? I've given you loads of examples, so take 60 seconds and give me 5 or 10 answers to each question on that *sixth* piece of paper.

Toolset Seven - Avoid These

This final toolset focuses on things to *avoid*. These are things that, in excess, can bring your energy down.

Let's begin with alcohol.

I think the first beer or glass of wine is absolutely fine. It seems relaxes you somewhat. That sounds good! And maybe the second one is OK too.

However, when you go too far, your energy plummets. If you drink a whole bottle of Jack Daniels on your own, chances are your energy is low and your creativity has gone out the window.

The same is true of drugs. Drugs are also on the list to avoid. Some of my musician friends need something to relax before the creativity flows, so they have some medical marijuana. At least, that's what they tell me! I presume it's medical. Anyway – the first joint seems fine. The problem is the second, third, fourth or fifth joint that robs them of their motivation. They seem to just sit around and giggle – which is fine but not helping write their next album!

Of course, there are some non-physical energy sappers, too. Television is among these. The first hour of television, as you giggle your way through an episode of The Big Bang Theory, seems fine. It's when you're spending 11 hours a day watching television that you might want to start asking questions.

Also, you must consider the quality of television you're watching. If you feed your mind with the fear and pain featured in the news networks, then fear and pain will pervade your thoughts. If you spend your time watching graphic depictions of murder, death and violence, those too will feature in your mind's eye. While those things are stimulants in moderation, an endless diet has energetic implications.

You must, therefore, ask yourself *'What is an ideal balance for me?'*

Exercise Seven – Your Things to Avoid

OK. Please put down the book and grab your next page. Write the words 'Things to Avoid' at the top of the page, and then answer this question –

What things should I avoid?

What are your personal answers to this question? I've given you loads of examples, so take 60 seconds and give me 5 or 10 answers to each question on that *last* piece of paper. What are your toxins? List your 5 or 10 toxins to avoid, toxins that suck your energy.

Your Toolbox

OK – all the exercises are done! Now we've covered seven toolsets.

- how you fuel your body,

- how you move your body,

- where you are,

- who you're with,

- what you're listening to,

- what colors surround you, and

- what your personal rituals are.

We also made some notes on what to avoid.

Those are seven groups of things you can do to manage your energy. If you've done 10 entries for each, you should now have dozens of different tools you can use to get you into your optimum state.

From here, it's as simple intentionally bringing your tools into your day. You could add good music to your morning routine, for example. You could book some calls and meetings with energy surplus people into your day. Working with one of my CEO clients, we've actually asked his personal assistant to meet with him briefly every week to make sure his energy tools are worked into his calendar. Maybe you could talk to a friend for a few minutes every morning and help each other bring an energetically aware mind set in your day.

After a while, it'll become second nature.

When you're feeling down, instead of trying to *soldier on* or *push through,* you'll come to realize that it's time to deploy some of your many tools to raise your energy. When your energy is better, you'll be back to optimal state for every aspect from work to play to going on a hot date. Easy!

Aspect #4

MIND SOUP

Creativity and Innovation

PETE COULD ONLY DELIVER

IF HE IMPOSED ARTIFICIAL DEADLINES.

Aspect #4 - Mind Soup

Calling a section of this book 'Mind Soup' is admittedly a little confusing. What on earth could Mind Soup possibly be?

Mind Soup is my name for the problem of trying be creative when your mind is full of distractions. Let me explain.

Your energy might be fantastic. You've had, for example, a great morning, good sleep, and you got up and ate high energy foods and drank good water. Maybe you went for a walk out in nature, maybe spoke to an energy surplus friend, and you're just feeling like you're on top of the world.

Sometimes, however, even if you do all of that - if your mind is full of rubbish, cluttered by negativity, fear and pain, or just general debris from the day, then creativity and innovative thoughts have *nowhere to land*. In other words, your mind is so full of useless thoughts your imagination has no room to play. The creative muse loves an empty mind!

The Soup Visualisation

Let's do a quick exercise. Imagine a can of Campbell's tomato soup. You know those cans, white bottom, red top. They've been the same way for many years. Next, imagine there's a shelf, in a cupboard or a pantry, that's exactly the height of one can of soup. Maybe it holds five cans across and two cans deep. Let's say you stock it up, with 10 cans, and let's say there are five shelves and you stock all of them up – five shelves and 10 in each, making 50 cans.

Now your imaginary pantry is completely full.

Now, imagine you have *just one more can of soup*.

Hang on – now you're stuck! There's simply nowhere left to put it. Unfortunately, you can't squeeze or bend or repack your cans in a different way. There's simply nowhere else for the soup to go.

In this analogy, *your mind is the pantry* and *your thoughts are the cans of soup*. And here's the problem – when your mind is full, when your pantry is full of tomato soup, you simply have nowhere left to put amazing new thoughts. So even when an amazing, creative, fantastic, innovative thought is knocking on your mind, busting to get in, if your mind is full, there's nowhere for it to land.

So what you need to do is *empty your mind*. If you can empty your mind, especially of thoughts that do not serve you, then there's room for inspiration. And every little bit helps! The best, of course, is a completely empty mind. It's when you have a totally empty mind that extraordinarily creative leaps seem to happen.

So how do you empty your mind? It turns out there's another amazing Eastern tradition with thousands of years of practice in doing just that one thing.

Using Meditation

For some, meditation looks like sitting in a cave, preferably in Tibet, surrounded by wastelands of ice and snow. For most of us, however, that sounds like hard work. Instead, we find meditation in different forms.

Apparently Steve Jobs used to go for long walks, just to empty his mind. He was a big meditator, which is probably the number one – with a bullet – best technique for emptying your mind. Other people find a meditative state at the gym, sipping on a cup of tea or even watching movies. I like to sit in a quiet place and let the extraneous thoughts simply flow out of my mind until there's nothing left.

Specifically, meditation is about dwelling in the gap between thoughts. It's about having the emptiest mind possible where there's absolutely nothing left except ... you. That's so powerful I'm going to repeat myself. The theory is when your mind is completely empty; whatever is left *must be you*. Trippy, right?

Most people's minds are full of debris. They're full of stories, usually about things from the past or the future. Most people are running stories about what just happened – "Oh gosh, that meeting was terrible, she hated me, she'll never work on that, I'll never get an approval for that," or "Wow, I've just left the house, did I really lock the door? I think maybe I better go back. No I don't have time. Did I leave something on the stove? Is the stove on? Is the whole house going to explode?" Or it's future – "Oh my goodness, I'm going to the dentist later this week. Is it going to be painful? Are there going to be fillings? Is it going to be expensive? Am I going to be able to afford it? And how about the rent?" On and on it goes.

Our minds are capable of dwelling endlessly on the past and worrying about the future. We fill up our mind's available "bandwidth" with stories that we feel we have to repeat again and again. Research was done in which it was proved that 97% of the thoughts you have today are *repeats of the thoughts you had yesterday.* That means most people are 97% simply repeats leaving only 3% of thoughts with the potential to be creative or new. What's going on in *your* mind?

Empty Your Mind

Everyone has a different way of emptying their mind. I like meditation but it's not for everyone. Some people walk on the beach, feed the cat, call their mum or let some music play.

Whatever it is that is your personal way of emptying your mind, I highly recommend you do it before you try and do something creative and innovative. Before you reach for your next amazing song or painting or sculpture, take a moment to empty your mind.

Exercise Eight – Emptying Your Mind

Let's do a quick exercise to write down some of your tools. In sixty seconds, white down the answer to the follow question -

What are the things that I do that empty my mind?

Is it meditation? Is it going to the gym? Is it watching a movie? Is it a walk by the beach? What do you do to empty your mind? List 5 or 10 things in the next 60 seconds. Go.

Aspect #5

CREATIVITY
PRACTICE

Creativity and Innovation

TOM HAD TOTALLY FAILED TO
PERSUADE HIS TEAM TO
THINK OUTSIDE THE BOX.

Aspect #5 – Creativity Practice

Next, let's focus on brain technology. In other words, if you want to be innovative and creative, you'd better know how to access the part of your brain that handles this. This is half of your brain, not all of your brain.

Your brain is split into two halves – the left brain and the right brain.

- The **left brain** is all about logic, reason, science, math, and linear process. It takes complex tasks and splits them carefully into smaller tasks so each gets done. It's to-do lists, it's rigorous process.

- The **right side** of your brain is about emotion, feeling, creativity and innovation. It's about connection to spirit or God or the muse. The right side is where paintings are painted, books are written, extraordinary business ideas come from, deep connections and relationships dwell.

Brain Sequencing

Knowing how your brain is constructed is really important for one reason. You see, the two sides of your brain *love to fight*. That's the ugly truth!

So here's the golden rule – **you cannot have your left brain and right brain in the same room at the same time.** Instead, you must work with them *in sequence*.

If you've ever been involved in a brainstorm, you know how this works. If you have 8 fantastically right-brained people in a great state, good energy, feeling creative and fantastic, and one left-brained person there to harpoon all of their ideas, it just doesn't work.

The right brain is really good at answering this question – **what?** What do we want? What's a great idea? What's a new cool connection? That's a terrific question to start with. Therefore, the right brain always goes first.

The left brain is good at answering this question – **how**? That's a terrific question to follow with. Therefore, the left brain must go second.

The key is to create a sequence: **right brain first, left brain second.** That's the first piece of brain sequencing technology; the importance of accessing the 2 sides of your brain in that specific linear order, never in parallel.

Mind Mapping

The second important piece of brain technology is mind mapping. For those who don't know, it's a method of taking notes invented by Tony Buzan. It's especially good in a brainstorming and creative situations because it keeps you in your right brain.

If you tried to use an Excel Spread-sheet as the note-taking method for your brainstorm, you'd find yourself going into your left brain even if you didn't want to. That's because Excel is laid out in a grid. It invites the left brain to think about which order things should be in, what the form and structure should be. This takes you out of your right brain.

Mind mapping is a system that imitates the way your mind is physically built. If you consider structure of your brain, it's made of highly connected neurons. In other words, your brain is a fantastic, complex mess of connections. It reflects the way you think: associatively. One idea brings another.

Well, mind mapping works just like that. You start off with an idea, or maybe a question. The question might be, *who are the characters in my book?* And then outside as ideas start to flow into your mind, you start to take notes and you connect them visually with links.

As you make your way into the detail of these ideas, you connect them further and further out on the page with more and more visual links. Whether you use words or images, it's a great way of making notes that are playful and inter connective and associative that replicates the way your brain is made and the way you think. So mind mapping is a great way to take notes during creative and innovative phases because it keeps you in the right brain.

A Mind Mapping Caveat

People frequently ask me should they mind map with pen and paper or on a computer, using mind mapping software. I like to use pen and paper because over time, they've become intuitive. I don't even notice I have a pen in my hand. I just write! I just think about what I want on the page and my body makes it happen. Easy.

Mind mapping software, on the other hand, tends to force your mind to focus on the technology itself. You must constantly click and drag and type. It is not intuitive. It does not happen subconsciously. In that way it is a less optimal system for mind mapping, in my experience.

Aspect #6

EXTERNAL
CREATIVITY

Creativity and Innovation

UGG MAY HAVE INVENTED THE WHEEL,

BUT BLATT INVENTED COPYRIGHT THEFT.

Aspect #6 - External Creativity

Even when you're doing everything right, even when

- your energy is fantastic,

- you're in a great place with good fuel and good people,

- you're not horribly drunk or stoned,

- you've used all the tools we mentioned, and

- your mind is empty –

- sometimes the right idea just doesn't surface.

So what do you do then? Where do you go for creativity when your own internal resources have come up short?

This is where the world has changed radically in the last couple of years.

Let's think back for a moment. Imagine you were the creative director at an advertising agency even five or ten years ago. If you wanted some great ideas for a campaign you simply went to your team. In fact, you prided yourself on having the best team in the business. If your team didn't come up with great ideas almost instantly, that was considered a failure.

Now, that way of thinking is becoming antiquated. The old question was *What is the best idea my team has?* The new question is be *How can I access the best ideas available?*

Now it is possible to simply, cheaply and easily access a global dynamic team to solve our problems as a collective. Whether you're a writer, a creative director, an artist, CEO or entrepreneur or anything in between, you can leverage this amazing new model of thinking. I've explained it in detail in other books – for now, I'll jump straight to the shortcuts relevant to the creative process.

Here are four places I go routinely to get new creative juice and great ideas fed to me. These fuel my own innovation and creativity or come to me as ready-made answers.

Fiverr.com

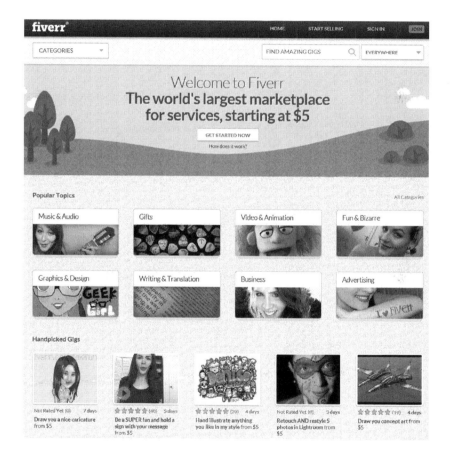

The first tool is a website called Fiverr.com. This website is absolutely crazy. It's the world's largest database of things you can get done for five dollars. You heard me – for the price of a cup of coffee you can access a global database of freelancers.

At first sight, you might think 'what could I get done for five dollars that I want to have done?' The answer is extraordinary things. So go ahead and log onto the website, and you'll see on the front page the first 10 or 20 random things they suggest you can get done for $5. And to be honest, when most people look at the front page, they are disgusted and throw up their hands and may log off and go find something else. That's because somehow, they generally list the stupidest, most ridiculous gigs on the front page. That's what they call a five-dollar job, by the way, a gig.

Ignoring the Home Page

And fiverr.com definitely lists random and stupid on their home page, so we're going to ignore them after we've had a brief chuckle. On today's fiverr.com home page you can

- Get your logo written on someone's bottom, they'll send you a picture for $5

- Get a lovely girl to be your girlfriend on Facebook for a week for $5.

- Get someone to send you a crochet hat for $5

These things are *not* what you'd call useful for business, and certainly not for creativity and innovation. It's not until you start searching the database that you find the extraordinary support for creativity and innovation.

Looking Deeper

It's not until you dive deeper by browsing or searching the database that you'll come up with the gold. On today's fiverr.com you can

- Get someone to design a new logo for you for $5. It can be a logo for a book, an album, a band, a new product or service.

- Get someone to install a wordpress web site for you for $5.

- Get someone to transcribe 15 minutes worth of audio that you've spoken into your phone, outlining a new book or great campaign idea, for $5.

- You can get someone to be your brainstorm partner for $5.

- You can get someone to write a 1,000 word story for you for $5.

Whether it's a concept for a business or a new product or a

new service, whether it's an idea for a book cover or an album cover, or an idea for a painting, there are amazing artists on fiverr.com. I once commissioned a gig where I got someone to draw my father as a Superhero. There are amazing creative resources there. I did all of the character design for my latest children's book, *The Amazing Adventures of Butt Crack Jack*, through Fiverr gigs. You have hundreds of thousands of people who are designers, copywriters, artists of every stripe, waiting to work for you for five dollars a time. It's a creative mecca and it's available to you 24/7 for the price of a sandwich.

Another strength of Fiverr.com is that it's international. Even if you think you've thought of everything, you probably haven't thought of your problem or your creative need from the point of view of somebody in France, or Latvia, or Serbia or Australia, or New Zealand.

Seriously, there are amazing people from all around the world, waiting to do things for you for five dollars. It's an extraordinary source of innovation and creativity.

For a video on Fiverr visit http://www.timlevy.net/fiverr or scan this QR code.

Elance.com

If you want a job bigger than Fiverr will allow, you move over to a website called Elance.com. Elance is a massive international database of freelancers of every stripe. Loads of creatives hang out there, whether it's writers, artists, designers, whether it's web designers or designers for book covers; they're all hanging out at Elance.com by the hundreds of thousands. In February 2013 alone, over 100,000 different jobs (and each might only be a task that takes a few hours or a couple of weeks) were done through Elance.

There are plenty of other sites competing with Elance, too. There are sites like Odesk or Freelancer or the Mechanical Turk.

I like Elance, and the thing is this: if you're looking for ideas, you just post a job and people who have great ideas or want to work for you come back and pitch for your business. They'll pitch not only what they'll do, what skills they have, and a portfolio of existing work, but also how much it's going to cost you. In a few hours can find 10 or 20 people who might be a resource for a creative project.

- You need a book written? You'll find ghost-writers on Elance.

- You need a logo designed? Elance.

- You need a website design? They're on Elance.

- You need ideas for an ad campaign? They're on Elance.

- You need 3D animation or video editing? They're on Elance.

- You need some awesome comedy? You'll find your comedian on Elance.

Creatives of every kind are waiting on Elance, waiting to help you. I generally hire people for between $50 and $250 doing quite major projects It's an extraordinary resource.

A Funny Story

Let me give you a real life example. I'm always using Elance. I have around three dozen people working for me routinely on Elance. I have writers, editors, animators – you name it. I even get my book keeping done through Elance.

In this case, however, I needed to write _a funny story_. Now I'm pretty comfortable writing stories but true comedy is a rare skill – or so I thought. I posted the following ad on Elance.

Comedy Writer / Scriptwriter Needed for Corporate Animated Shorts

Hello!

I'm looking for someone fun and easy to work with on a series of short animations for a corporate client. These are so-called 'conversion videos' for a web site, in the style of... say... the videos you'd find at Grumo. Once the scripts are written, we'll have them made into highly visual, quirky, funny and engaging short animations. Make sense?

Each one will be the story of a profile character with the business *being an answer to the problem scenario, followed by a gentle call to action.*

I'll start by hiring you for one script that will come to 2-3 minutes of animation. All going well, we have several more to do. Oh - and we're not a Fortune 100 company with wildly deep pockets - so be nice!

Ideally you'll have a strong portfolio full of short scripts that are going to make me burst out laughing. You might have a past in improv and stand-up. Certainly you'll have years of writing creds and your work has probably been made into TV, film or other published forms. Phew! You've been busy.

So! If that sounds like you, let's talk. I like to speak via Skype before I hire people to make sure we're a match. I also like to see a portfolio of existing work in written or video form.

With my thanks,

Tim

Here's what happened. Within three hours I had five experienced comedians applying for the job. Within 3 days I had nineteen. And these weren't kidding around – these were serious professional comedians with exactly the kind of experienced I'd asked for! And the asking price? They nominated prices on their own ranging from *$100-$200.* I hired an amazing comedian with 25 years experience, 4 film credits and corporate experience with brands like Coke, Wal-Mart and GE. His name is Dan and he's waiting on Elance for you!

For a video on Elance visit http://www. timlevy.net/elance or scan this QR code.

99Designs.com

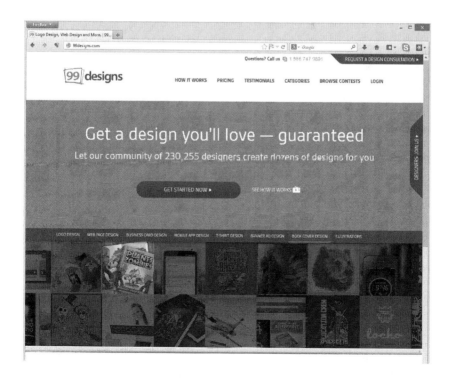

Let's look at a third web site, which is a bit more specific in the world of design. It's called 99Designs.com. Really, this is an extraordinary way of working creatively. Let's say you want something designed – could be a t-shirt, a business card, a letterhead; it could be a book cover, a logo, really anything you need designed.

Now normally you would start by trying to find an artist. You source a graphic designer, you look at their work, find one you like and they come back with two or three ideas for you. What you're limited to there is the creativity from a single mind. Those artists will only give you one person's ideas, with their style, preferences, comfort zone and background and experiences.

What if you wanted more than that? When you go to 99Designs. com, the process works differently. You suggest the amount of a prize, say $300 or $500 or $800, and then artists from anywhere in the world who want to help you compete for the prize. So you might put $500 there and have 50 different artists do three ideas each. So suddenly you have 100, 200, 400 different logo ideas. Now you get to work with the whole swarm, telling them what you like, what you don't like, until you pick the one you love. That individual wins the cash prize.

Web sites like 99designs.com give you extraordinary access to innovation and creativity at a sensational price.

For a video on 99designs visit http://www. timlevy.net/99 or scan this QR code.

DeviantArt.com

We've got three paid tools so far:

- Fiverr.com, where everything costs five bucks and you can get creativity on anything.

- Elance.com, which might be a bit more, maybe a couple of hundred dollars at a time, but then you might get someone to edit your book or write your book. Extraordinary creativity is accessible there.

- 99Designs.com, which is focused on design.

What about something that is more purely artistic? And what about something free?!

The place I like to go is DeviantArt.com. The name sort of says it all, but it's the world's largest database of artists. There are almost 250 million pieces of art on that site, in a searchable database. Almost 25 million artists are members. This is my one stop source for crazy cool and lateral creativity, because this artistic database is *searchable by keyword.*

You simply type in 'happy' and a thousand artistic interpretations of the word happy pop up. You type in 'shoes' and a thousand photos, web designs, paintings and sculptures with shoes in them pop up. Seriously. It's mind boggling.

Re-inventing Coffee

Once I was helping an advertising agency executive with a campaign to sell coffee. The problem is that coffee ads have been done every which way. Coffee has been around for ages. You've seen these TV ads of people waking up in the morning, smelling the coffee? It's been advertised forever.

So how do you come up with something truly creative and new? Well, we just started typing random words into DeviantArt and of course we typed in "coffee", "feeling better", "smell", "food"; we typed in "morning", and thousands of images started to emerge.

There was a new *font* that someone had created using coffee cup stains. Wow. What a fresh idea! There was an image of coffee as a binary switch turning humans on and off, suggesting a cool digital robot theme. Amazing. There was a picture of a coffee cup with a set of brass knuckles as the handle, entitled 'Coffee for tough guys'. Another amazing lateral idea.

Long story short, we were able to solve the agency's problem in a brief session using deviantart.com as a trigger for creative new ideas.

Of course if you'd like to work with the artists on the site, it only takes a moment to email them and invite them into your world. They always love being 'discovered'! If this happens, you can pursue the artwork with the artist and actually pay them for their art, or maybe have them help you work on your campaign. Or you can just use it as inspiration. It's a wonderful community of artists helping one another.

So there you are, four fantastic tools to outsource creativity if your own doesn't quite get you where you want to go.

IT'S A WRAP

Creativity and Innovation

It's a Wrap!

So there you have it from tip to tail – all the concepts, tools and processes you need to get into your optimal high-energy creative and innovative state and stay there. And if your true genius is on holiday, you can always outsource! Here's a quick summary of what we've covered.

- We started off with the **math**: energy equals clarity equals creativity. In other words, if your energy is high, your creativity is high. If your energy is low, your creativity is low.

- We looked at the **energetic spectrum** and described life and creative potential in positive, neutral and negative energetic states. Your optimal states for creativity and innovation live at positive energy levels. Feelings of fogginess, anxiety and uncertainly dwell at negative energy levels.

- We went into a set of seven toolsets – **fuel, movement, location, people, sound and color, ritual and things to avoid** – and you did a bunch of **exercises** where you came up with your own answers, not just parroting mine, for your own ways to manage your personal energetic level.

- We then moved into **mind soup**, helping clear a space in mentally in which inspiration and creativity can most easily land.

- We then went into how your **brain works** – splitting it into left and right brain, understanding that right brain and left brain don't work well together, but they work well in sequence, used one after another. The right brain comes first, to figure out what your ideas are, and the left brain comes second, to figure out how to implement them in the real world.

- We went into **mind mapping** that keeps you in the right brain, as a good tool for taking notes and keeping records of your creativity.

- After optimizing your personal innovation and creativity, we went even further. We went beyond what you can do on your own and found 4 fantastic places to **outsource creativity**.

  - **Fiverr.com** is where you can get things done for five dollars at a time.

  - **Elance.com** is one of the world's largest databases of freelancers from all over the world who have extraordinary creativity at your fingertips.

  - **99Designs.com** is where you start to crowd source your creativity.

  - **DeviantArt.com** is an extraordinary creative community of artists in which you can inspire and be inspired, connecting with extraordinary minds the world over.

During the book, you also encountered links back to my web site where there are various free videos and further information to help you implement everything in this book.

Is there more I can do?

If there's any way I can help you further, then let's talk. Please call, email me directly or via *Contact Us* on the site I'll see what I can do.

Tim Levy and Associates LLC

Based In | Austin, Texas

Telephone | (512) 782 4401

Email | creativity@timlevy.net

Web | www.timlevy.net

Quick Links

Here is a quick list of all the links mentioned in the book.

- http://www.timlevy.net/gdtv for my TV pastt

- http://www.timlevy.net/money for information on the Energy of Money program

- http://www.timlevy.net/fiverr for a video on Fiverr

- http://www.timlevy.net/elance for a video on Elance

- http://www.timlevy.net/99 for a video on 99 Designs, and

- http://www.timlevy.net for more information, books and programs.

Other Recent Titles Include ..

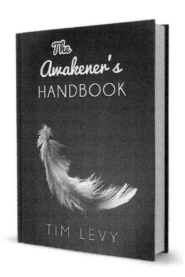
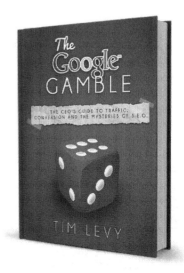
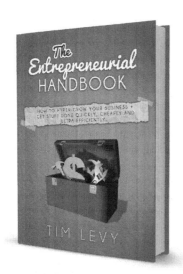
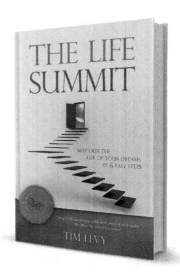

Available online at www.timlevy.net

Made in the USA
Lexington, KY
20 May 2014